# MEDITATION, DEFINING *your* SPACE

Elizabeth Banfalvi

**BALBOA.**
PRESS

A DIVISION OF HAY HOUSE

Balboa Press books may be ordered through booksellers or by contacting:

Balboa Press
A Division of Hay House
1663 Liberty Drive
Bloomington, IN 47403
www.balboapress.com
1 (877) 407-4847

Because of the dynamic nature of the Internet, any web addresses or links contained in this book may have changed since publication and may no longer be valid. The views expressed in this work are solely those of the author and do not necessarily reflect the views of the publisher, and the publisher hereby disclaims any responsibility for them.

The author of this book does not dispense medical advice or prescribe the use of any technique as a form of treatment for physical, emotional, or medical problems without the advice of a physician, either directly or indirectly. The intent of the author is only to offer information of a general nature to help you in your quest for emotional and spiritual well-being. In the event you use any of the information in this book for yourself, which is your constitutional right, the author and the publisher assume no responsibility for your actions.

Any people depicted in stock imagery provided by Thinkstock are models, and such images are being used for illustrative purposes only.
Certain stock imagery © Thinkstock.

Printed in the United States of America.

ISBN: 978-1-4525-1612-7 (sc)
ISBN: 978-1-4525-1611-0 (e)

Library of Congress Control Number: 2014909848

Balboa Press rev. date: 06/06/2014

Change is what makes life interesting. Being
able to change makes it worthwhile.
*Elizabeth Banfalvi www.elizabethbanfalvi.com*

# Contents

Introduction ..................................................................... ix

Helpers ........................................................................... xi

Perceptions ..................................................................... xii

A Higher Order ............................................................. xiv

Journaling ..................................................................... xvi

Nature .......................................................................... xix

Themes ............................................................................ 1

    Meditation Themes ................................................ 3

    Ceremonies ............................................................ 7

    Rituals .................................................................... 9

    Altars ...................................................................... 11

Elements ........................................................................ 13

    Elements ................................................................. 15

    Element Uses .......................................................... 17

    Element Meditations .............................................. 19

    Astrology and the Elements ................................... 21

    Astrology Meditations ............................................ 23

Numbers ........................................................................ 25

    Numbers and Their Meanings ................................ 27

    Cards and Their Meanings ..................................... 29

    Lucky Bamboo Stalks ............................................. 32

Time & Directions ........................................................ 35

    Time Captured ....................................................... 37

    Portions of Time .................................................... 38

    Directions and Belief Systems ................................ 40

Vibrations ......................................................... 45
    Colors and Their Meanings.............................. 47
    Candles and Ambiance ................................... 50
    The Power of Scents ....................................... 53
    Music of the Soul............................................ 57

Crystals, Gems and Metals.................................. 59
    Crystal Uses.....................................................61
    Crystals Cleansing ......................................... 63
    Crystals, Gems and Metals ............................. 66

Meditations...................................................... 71
    A New Direction ........................................... 73
    Celebrations – Time ...................................... 75

Final Thoughts.................................................. 77
Glossary of Meditations .................................... 79

# Introduction

This book is about defining your space and using helpers to make it personal, comfortable or whatever you want to feel. Helpers are a way to make your meditations become easier and more interesting. They are a way of finding connections with nature and different aspects. It is also a journey of awakening in a different way. It is a way to focus and have fun but bring a novel way to change your meditations.

When you begin to meditate it is can be difficult to just sit and try to rid your mind of all the different thoughts you have running around in your head. But if you can physically hold an object then your focus is on the object and the physicality of it. The roughness of a crystal, or a pine cone or the softness of a feather can help you concentrate and direct your thoughts better.

There are helpers in nature, Native American culture, Feng Shui, crystals, colors, music and so many varied ways to help you concentrate on what you are focusing on. Introduce time into your meditations and it can be an ally. Use the many meaningful holidays, seasons, days and months as a focus. You can use the beginning of the day to introduce yourself to a new way of thinking or to make a new beginning. At the end of the day, you can find a completion in how you are feeling and know that in the morning, you can begin again in newness.

In life, there is a continuous cycle of beginnings and endings and that is a natural process. Everything has a cycle.

This book is full of information and different aspects which can be used in a multitude of ways. Not all the information will be what you want to use and that is perfectly alright. Use what feels right and experiment in other things. This book is about presenting ideas and novel ways to enhance your meditation process. The internet has more information if you want to investigate more in depth than what I have offered. Use all things in a positive context and you will find what works for you.

Have fun doing all sorts of things and try as many as you can. I always instruct my class to use what you need when you need it and then let it go. Learn to use helpers but also learn to let them go to be able to connect all by yourself. You can still use them but don't become dependent on them.

Included in this book is a glossary of meditations which lists my meditations from my previous books. Everything that is presented in this book can be adapted or used in any meditation.

Take the time to enjoy the journey.

# Helpers

Helpers are simply about making your meditation more interesting and varied. Most people probably think meditation is just about sitting, focusing your mind, and relaxing. Meditation can be so much more than that. At times, it can be about relaxing and increasing your focus, but you can use your meditation to guide and help you in so many other ways.

You can use meditation to help you change your life and attitude. You can change your energy or recharge it. You can change your focus or refocus on something you want to accomplish within your life. You can begin again and release what you perceive has been holding you back.

For example, if you want a change in your life, do your meditations at the beginning of the day. Use the beginning of the day to meditate and highlight what you want to change in your life. You will also find that the new moon is all about beginnings, so celebrate the new moon in your meditations. In the fall, it is all about planting the seeds for your new life, so celebrate that season to begin the year and project the direction you want to go in your life. Journal the direction you want to go—the feelings you want and the changes you want to project in your life. Physically writing it down makes it more solid, and you can look back on it as you grow with each day.

Your meditations are very personal and can help in many various ways, which in turn can help your everyday life be more fulfilling. This is about enhancing your power and using tools to help you. The operative word is "help", because you already have the power to do it yourself. Train yourself to use what you need, to get you where you want to go.

# Perceptions

Whenever you are using helpers in your meditations, no matter what they are, be aware of how you feel or perceive them. What feels good to one person doesn't necessarily feel good to another. Be aware of your surroundings and all the accessories you use.

Music is very personal and can add a beautiful dimension to your meditations, but some people prefer quiet. If you have a favorite song or maybe a classical piece, use it, but be aware, some music doesn't translate well to your meditation. If there is a voice on it, be aware of the sound of the voice and if you are getting the effect you want.

Crystals are very interesting and have a wonderful history. Get a variety of them, and use them in your practice. Look into their different uses and qualities. You can get smaller ones and keep them close to you or at your workstation; only you will know they are there and what their significance is. I am not a great crystal worker, but when I was going through a difficult time, I looked up crystals that would give me strength. I used them constantly, and they helped me and gave me a feeling that I was being strengthened and wasn't alone in my struggles.

If nature is what gives you the qualities you want in your meditation, use it. If you are intrigued with native Indians and their beliefs, seek them out and work with their drums, chants, and other parts of their belief systems.

If you love candles, use them. There are different colors, meanings and scents that entice the feelings. There are also different shapes and sizes. If you like tea lights, you can get a holder for them. If you like a larger, thicker candle, use those. If you like the taper kind, again use what you like—it is your choice and your feelings that are most important. It is about creating a wonderful atmosphere or ambiance so you enjoy your meditation.

Try using positive affirmations, card decks, calendars, sayings, prayers, poetry, and literature to give you a different slant on what you are doing. Choose what appeals to you and gives you a sense of something different, whether it is feeling positive, recharging, life-changing, or balancing yourself.

What appeals to you will help you to perceive a different feeling or encouragement. It is about helping you come back and meditate on a regular basis. Your perception on what you are using will change because you grow and change, so always be aware if what you use is still giving you the feeling you want. If it isn't, then change it. Welcome newness on a regular basis, and try what works for someone else; maybe it will work and maybe it won't, but have fun with it.

Be aware, and give honor to your perceptions, because they are there to help you.

# A Higher Order

Whether you are religious or not, some people believe in a way of living which involves a higher order of life. Some others might not believe in this and again that is the way it is. There are all different beliefs which are intrinsic to the individual. Either way, religions usually have certain icons or belief systems and symbolic articles like a bible, cross, or other symbols.

When you are meditating, all of this can be very helpful to incorporate into your meditations. It brings a higher sense of order to what you are doing. I have been christened in the United Church, and my mother was Roman Catholic, so a picture of Jesus was always present along with a bible and a cross. I know the Lord's Prayer and also Hail Mary, which are Catholic prayers. I believe in these religious symbols and they bring me comfort. I have attended both Catholic and United Church services. I also christened my children in the United Church. Although I don't attend church on a regular basis, it is still what I believe in.

Even with my grandchildren, I gave them a sense of something higher than what we are. I talk to them about using prayers, for example, as comfort when they are troubled. My mother taught me when I was having nightmares to get up and put a sign of the cross on my pillow and then lay my head in the middle. After doing that, I used to fall asleep easily. It is a sense of something in a comforting, protective mode that we can turn to in times of trouble to ask for help. I frequently send up prayers for guidance and help and then send up prayers of gratitude for what I have been given or for just knowing I am connected. I truly believe there is something beyond us and I would never want to think there wasn't.

In your meditations, you can choose to use this higher power to aid in what you desire no matter if you are a specific religion. There are many sources to find out what you can incorporate. There are series of cards that have saints and guardian angels on them and sayings to go with each of them. You can access websites that talk about angels, religious icons, and symbols, so you can find out about them and see what brings you comfort. No religion, to me, is a standalone but a part of each other in their beliefs—to believe in the goodness of a higher order and the moral values we all have. If you don't know what you believe in, then find a variety of symbols and incorporate them.

# Journaling

Journaling is a wonderful way to capture your life in your own words. It is a way of remembering how far your journey has taken you and where you wish to travel. We have a tendency to forget how we felt or what we were doing before we started changing or growing. It gives us a way of recognizing the beginnings of our everyday journey. It may not seem important, but it helps us be aware of our accomplishments and the various ways we have improved. Nothing that is worth living is a waste, and we always grow within our troubled or happy times.

There are various types of journals, and the ones suggested here will be simple ones to get you started on your journey. I believe hand writing your journal when you begin is very effective. There are different ways you can actually enter your journals on a computer, but the effort it takes to hand write your journal takes a different energy than typing out your words. To feel the words flowing through the movement of your hand on paper is much more personal, and you can feel the movement of the pen or pencil forming the letters. If you are unable to hand write your journals, go ahead and use whatever method you want, but feel the energy in the forming of your words.

My friend, who originally did my hardcover book art, journals through his art rather than writing words. He expresses himself through art. My original "Hectic" book cover was a combination of several drawings he had already done. When he went through a very difficult time in his life, he used a journal where he drew daily. He drew simple things that surrounded him. It helped him relax and gave him an outlet for his feelings.

Begin by finding a journal you enjoy, with either lined or plain paper inside. Find a color, texture, and shape you like. If using the cover with inserts, find a cover matching the insert's size and then add texture to your journal by adding tab inserts or a book marks. Find a writing tool you like to use and hold as you write. Keep the journal in a place where you can access it easily. Make a point of writing in it each day. Always date your entries.

One purpose of your journal could be that you are going through a difficult time in your life or a loss of a loved one, job or relationship. Begin by writing about how you feel and date the entry. This is your personal journal so write down all of your feelings because nobody will see it but you. Don't worry about grammar or being technically correct – this is just about where you are right now. Be honest with yourself and tell yourself what worked and what didn't. If this was a loss or death, what are your new responsibilities? Next imagine yourself at a better place and what it will take to get there. What do you need to fulfill your dreams? Now as difficult as it seems, end it by saying at least 3 positive things you are grateful for today. Each day, pick something new to be grateful for. Now close your journal and set it aside.

You can have more than one journal so maybe another journal could be to help you change the direction of your life. Begin by writing down where you are at this present time. Write down your goals, hopes, wishes, dreams and the qualities you want to feel when you have achieved your goals. Write down what qualities you have now and what steps you have to take in order to achieve your goals. You can include pictures or visuals about what you want to achieve. Again write down 3 positive things you are grateful for. Adjust your goals as needed when you start achieving them. Add more goals you want to achieve because time changes what you believe can happen so open yourself up for more and leave an opening for unexpected treasures.

Whatever your reason will be for a journal, keep a consistency in them and end by writing down positive grateful things. No matter how simple or extensive your journal is, the importance is in how you will relate to yourself when you see your written word. It will be very interesting when you can see where and how you have changed. It can be used as a mirror for reflection in an honest way. Use it in a positive way so that you can change your life and see the changes you have made. You will be surprised at the transformation in yourself.

Be defined in your journal by following these rules:

1. Date your entries
2. Be free with your feelings and where you are at the present
3. Don't restrict yourself to what you think a journal is about, it's yours
4. Be honest with yourself
5. Be grateful
6. Look forward and believe in yourself
7. Enjoy what you do and praise yourself and your accomplishments

# Nature

Nature and all its seasons are part of who we are. In fall, we start gathering and dressing warmer and wearing richer colors. In winter, we tend to slow down and spend more time at home. In spring, we burst forth and welcome the sun and start wearing brighter colors and shinier jewelry. In summer, our clothes again change and we blossom in the sun, turning to the rays whenever we can. We lengthen our days to take advantage of the sunlight. We do so naturally because we are nature and part of the earth.

Nature is very helpful if we want to simplify our lives and to help ground ourselves when we are feeling scattered. Taking a walk in nature seems to clear our minds and helps us to feel more centered. Walk among the trees, flowers or foliage – all the green and natural colors surround us, and we breathe in the scents of nature all around us. We are able to feel the trees large and thick forming homes for the birds, squirrels and other nature creatures. We walk in the sunlight, the rain, the morning dew or the evening mist.

Using water, we feel we can immerse ourselves in water whether an ocean or bath. We can feel it supporting us as in the womb as being surrounded by liquid – giving us a feeling of floating and being sustained. We shower and feel the water cascade down our body allowing us to feel released. We feel refreshed when we bathe in a whirlpool or a misty spa. We feel expansiveness when we look at the ocean, or we can imagine floating like a leaf down a gurgling brook. We can imagine feeling the depth of a lake surrounded by large mountains. We can feel the power of the ocean waves hitting the shore over and over again spraying up each time. We naturally raise our face to the snowflakes cold and gentle on our face. There are so many things we can do in the snow. We can scrunch through the deep snow, form snow angels or make snowballs.

We see the beautiful sky with clouds and imagine what the clouds are shaped like. We see the thunderclouds and the lightning breaking through the clouds frightening and yet so majestic. We feel the crackle in the air and smell the impending rain. We see the many colors of the sunset and then the subdued ones of the sunrise slowly lighting the sky. We see the moon clear and bright or large and suspended above the horizon, round and golden. The stars light the moonless sky and form a canopy above us.

These are the things you can bring into your meditations either physically or mentally. Bring some colorful autumn leaves or fresh spring flowers into your meditation. Walk in the crisp fall air renewing your feelings. Gather different sea shells or rocks by the lake or ocean and feel your world expanding. Feel the sunrise beginning your day and the sunset ending or feel the dawning of new feelings or life's direction and the completion of what you no longer need.

Pick different things in nature to bring renewed feelings into your meditations. Use what is familiar and suits what is going on in your life. Nature reflects your life and you can use those qualities.

# Themes

# Meditation Themes

One of the focus points you can use in your meditation is incorporating a theme. It could be personal, a new direction or a global theme. There are many global organizations which set up meditation circles. It does settle the world and lessens turmoil when millions of people are concentrating on the same positive theme at the same time. Search them out and see what you can get involved in. You can also form a global theme yourself when there are natural or unnatural incidents or disasters going on.

The best way to incorporate a theme is to pinpoint and focus on an issue that is relevant to you. Think about it and write it down. Hold it, hang it at eye level or keep it close by while meditating so that your focus stays on the theme. Surround yourself with objects which represent the theme and incorporate some colors, crystals or sayings. Below are some themes which can be used over and over again and a suggested affirmation. Journal at each step as you change your life no matter how small it is. Pay attention to changes.

Some pointers to incorporate are:

1. Incorporate a theme (keep it simple and then adjust)
2. Keep it positive
3. Assume a positive outcome
4. Use helpers to keep the focus
5. Give it a timeline if possible
6. Be patient

**Health**: health is a big issue in our lives because there are times when our health isn't the optimum it can be. Use an affirmation which states that you are in great health already rather than focusing on the sickness. If you are focusing on someone else's health, then you must start with yourself and then when feeling the best send the healing energy to others. At the end come back to yourself and help yourself.

**Affirmation**: I am healthy.

**Prosperity**: this isn't about money or being rich because that is a perception of wealth. To be prosperous means to be able to afford where you are at the present time. Then as you progress, you will feel the prosperity at every higher level. You have to love where you are so that you can love where you will eventually be. Prosperity isn't about owning but enjoying what you do own now.

**Affirmation**: I am prosperous in every way.

**Changes**: we all need changes in our lives and they happen constantly. We must embrace changes and welcome them because they are a natural part of who we are. They happen even when we don't want them to. You can focus on change or incorporate the changes that are already happening so that you can understand it better. Changes can sometimes seem as roadblocks but see them as lessons along the way. Roadblocks can help us change direction and then open our lives up to possibilities.

**Affirmation**: I change easily and go in the best direction in my life.

**Relationships**: our relationships are always changing and that is how it should be. We are all unique and we come into each other's lives to help motivate and/or strengthen who we are. When asking about relationships, know who you are so that you bring what serves you better. We tend to draw a level of who we are to our lives, so learn from that. Look at the people who surround you and see them as a mirror.

**Affirmation**: I have amazing relationships and they enhance my life.

**Global**: global issues can be either healing a war zone, a natural disaster or some other global chaos. If there is an event in a certain country or something that affects an ethnic population, focus on the event and send a peaceful healing energy. Pick a positive energy to transmit and feel it going forward. You can light a candle to send light forward to the event. At times, it might be useful to have a group which is like-minded to help you. Get as much information as possible and set up the event as a ceremony that you can all contribute to. Ask the members to contribute other issues you can help on a go-forward basis. Always remember to acknowledge your own community or country.

**Affirmation**: I send positive energy to the world to help it heal.

**New career path/direction**: at times, there needs to be a change in your life which will fulfill a different direction for you. List the positive aspects of the new direction that you want to have. List the aspects, location, prosperity level, creativity, and all aspects that need to be considered. Keep the list updated and change anything that doesn't appeal to you as you go forward in your meditations. Keep your focus active. Also what is good is to release what you are presently active in. You have to release the old to replace it with the new.

**Affirmation**: I have a great career and direction in my life. I improve my life constantly.

**Endings/Beginnings**: in life at times, there has to be an end to have a beginning. At times, we can choose the endings but not always. A death can and does happen and eventually it will be someone we know. A job can end or a time of your life or relationships ends. There are many wonderful ceremonies you can incorporate to celebrate/honor the endings. I did say to celebrate/honor. When we accept an end, we can appreciate what we had so that we can begin again. We can never truly recapture what has ended but we can build on it as a foundation. Burning a candle and writing the ending down on a piece of a paper is very liberating. Thank the ending and what it has brought you whether it was positive or negative. Then honor it by burning it in the candle flame and watching it burn. Watch the paper become burnt ashes and then imagine the newness rise out of the ashes.

**Affirmation**: I easily accept endings and welcome new beginnings.

As you can see there are traditional themes you can use but there are many more. When you go for a theme, if you want, you can pull a tarot, angel or other type of cards to help you create energy around the theme. Use times of the day, moon cycles or seasons to help create the theme. Be aware of the cycles in your life because you do change naturally. Create a picture around the theme you have chosen. Then enjoy the results of your meditations.

# Ceremonies

Ceremonies are used to highlight or recognize special accomplishments and goal attainment. They are for celebrations, themes, endings, beginnings and all types of different events. Use them in your meditations when you need to mark a time of your life that is important either as a celebration or an ending. Always give importance to these times.

Ceremonies can be used:

- To convey a message or lesson.
- To inspire you to reach greater heights in your personal growth.
- To convey that "you" and "this moment" are special.

Organize your celebration in this manner:

- **Introduction:** Pick a theme and keep focus on your theme or purpose throughout the ceremony.
- **Body:** Be aware of the development of your theme and how to progress with it. Use different props within the meditation to help the theme along e.g. pictures, sayings, affirmations, cards, poetry, etc.
- **Climax or Summary:** Project forward to what you want and the timeframe, if there is an achievement with it. At the last, be grateful and include highlights of the developments. The more you honor the process, the more it will give you fulfilment.

To achieve these goals, a ceremony must be more than a ritual; it must be a communication of thoughts and feelings. The ceremony must say something that matters.

**Theme:** A concept or idea around which the ceremony is built. It is most effective when they can be linked to something current or to an issue that will relate to you.

**Focus:** A center of focus is a must in creating a meaningful ceremony. The center of activity should contain a symbolic feature or simple object to catch and hold your attention. Actions performed during the ceremony should be simple and occur around the focal point.

**Setting:** The nature of the occasion will help to determine the place and atmosphere that is best suited for the particular ceremony. Take advantage of the area where the ceremony is held. Be creative!

**Dramatic Effects:** Use of dramatic effects can be a real asset to any ceremony. Swelling the music, lowering the lights, lighting candles, starting a campfire, getting the flag to ripple in the breeze of a fan, uncovering an object on a table, building a model, and many other simple, easy gestures can catch the attention.

**Ending:** The ending is just as important as the beginning. Design it to compliment the whole program and help reinforce the message in your mind and heart. When the ending begins, it should be obvious that the special moment is complete. Use an effect to end the ceremony. For example, if candles are used, extinguish them at the close of the ceremony.

Ceremonies can be wonderful to implement in your life. It can also heighten the effect of your meditations and the times of your life. Use ceremonies to celebrate relevant times, solstices, or even moon phases. Celebrate your life.

# Rituals

A ritual is described as "a detailed method of procedure that is faithfully or regularly followed". Rituals are used in a multitude of ways. For this writing, we will talk about the use of rituals in the meditative process.

It isn't essential to make a ritual for your meditations but it helps when you are beginning to learn to meditate. Rituals make meditation a process rather than just an exercise. There are many aspects you can bring in as a ritual which will prompt you.

Rituals can help commit you to your meditations and make it more consistent. In a ritual, there is a setting up which uses time, place, surroundings and a form of Relaxation Response. In a ritual, you would have a beginning, middle and end very much like an unfolding and a refolding. Find a way of saluting the start and also the closing/finishing of your meditation.

You could have a favorite place or set-up an altar with personal meaningful articles. You can use a special rug, cushion or yoga mat. There could be a time that is favorable and can be adhered to on a regular basis, a time that is convenient for you. You can have a special covering that you use only in your meditations or a special sweater or robe. You can also incorporate a theme to your ritual. If you are having health related problems, make the ritual about bringing good health into your meditation. If you are seeking a career change, the ritual could be about bringing a new career direction and the feelings you want surrounding your new career. Use colors which enhance your theme.

Rituals are followed very closely in religion. Prayers are very powerful and religious symbols like crosses or prayer beads can be part of what you use.

The North American Native Indians use wonderful blessings to honor the earth and nature. They thank the earth and Mother Nature for supplying them with their needs. These blessings bring you more in contact with nature. Practice different methods and find what works for you. There are many sites you can access to find the different variations of prayers and blessings that can be used.

What is very useful is to also include gratitude in your meditative practice. Acknowledge what you are grateful for in your daily life no matter how small. A sense of gratitude will help you realize how blessed your life is. Journaling can also be an integral part of your meditations. Bring cherished items into your space and make it sacred to you and acknowledge them. Find items that relate to how you feel and change them whenever you feel like you need a change in them or a new energy. A picture of yourself when you were a child is very important to inspire innocence in your practice. If religion is important to you, keep religious items in your space. Find items, writings, or affirmations which add to your feelings of happiness or any emotions you are striving for in your meditation. Add items which are personal to you and incorporate nature which coincides to the season you are in. Bring nature into your space.

Eventually you will have your own rituals you will be comfortable with. They will help make you comfortable within your meditation practice. You will be able to meditate any place, time and for any reason and be very comfortable. Make your rituals comforting, safe, nurturing, protecting and personal.

# Altars

When you walk into a church or a religious place, usually you see front and center an altar which contains objects referring to the place and the practice which is being held in that location. An altar is used to display a place of sacredness. Nobody is usually allowed to touch it or remove the objects displayed.

An altar although it is used in churches and for religious ceremonies can be easily adapted to our meditative practice. It can be based on our religious or spiritual beliefs or can be totally different. It can be very elaborate or simple. Look around your place and see what your tokens of life are. Mine are flowers and plants and pictures of my grandchildren laughing or smiling broadly. I also have candles and knick knacks which are memory driven. So my altar would contain samples of this. I would also have, because I enjoy them, crystals, colorful items and probably a rosary although I'm not catholic. So what would you have on your altar?

Your altar might be very simple with maybe a simple cloth, a candle, a crystal which represents how you are feeling or want to feel and that would be it. Good for you. If this is what you want, then it is perfect. Some others might want so much more and that will be perfect for them. If it makes you feel good, then it is what you should have.

Your altar might also be on a small simple table which is low and close to the level you sit – perfect. You should easily see your altar because that is what it is there for. My advice is to make it symbolize who you are, how you want to be and how you want to see yourself. It should symbolize all of these things. Also remember that things and times change and so will your altar. Sometimes it will have more relevance and sometimes it won't.

Bring nature into it with all the seasons. Make it seasonal by adding things of nature. Bamboo shoots are easy to add and symbolize many things.

Check the other sections of this book for other ideas on what to add.

When you want to make your altar, use these steps.

Pick a place and locate it near where you meditate

1. Use some personal articles
2. Add nature
3. Incorporate your senses – touch (crystals), hear (cd), smell (scents), sight (color), feel (texture)
4. Add positive energy by imagining a white light surrounding your altar or add positive sayings
5. Make rituals around your altar – start and end by saying a prayer or a positive quotation, light a candle, add a reason or theme to your meditation, and incorporate some global wishes
6. Make it meaningful to you and your present situation
7. Keep it simple
8. Keep it consistent and timely

# Elements

# Elements

The four elements earth, water, fire and air are what we are discussing here. There is a fifth Chinese element, metal, which is in the Chinese tradition. These four represent the astrological signs and have symbolic traits. Earth is symbolic of being physical and of earthly pursuits. Water is symbolic of being able to flow with life and being more emotional. Fire is symbolic of being passionate and burning with emotions. Air is symbolic of freedom and being mentally active. Each has its own specific symbolic characterizations and can help you change the energy you feel. Use these elements and their traits within your meditations.

Earth is about being down to earth; on solid ground; shifting sands, etc. It teaches us that even if things shift in our lives there is still something solid beneath it. Earth is also about being solid but being soft, gentle and full of life. It is about not holding on too hard because it will trickle through your fingers like sand so loosen the hold. It is about burying the dead and planting new seeds. When you need to bring your world to a solid footing or you need to end something and then begin again, include earth, sand or a potted plant in your meditation area.

Water is about flowing with what is happening to you. It is one of the most valuable elements we have on this earth. Our oceans, rivers, streams, lakes and brooks are part of this. The rains and snow which fall on us from above keep our earth moist and encourages new growth. It is about our showers and baths which cleanse us. It is our tears cleansing our eyes and reflecting our sorrow and/or happiness. It is part of the flow of our body cleaning and sustaining it. When you need to flow with life, use the sound of water, a bottle of water or a picture of an ocean or lake.

Fire is all about passion and burning brightly. It is about being emotional and rising from the ashes after the burning away. It is about lighting the darkness, an eternal flame within us and the heat that warms us. When the fire is all over, we are left with ashes and like the Phoenix, we rise from the ashes. When you need to cleanse and start over again, or to promote passion in your life, use a candle, incense, a fire place or a picture of a flame to start again.

Air is about being able to mentally think it through or rise above it all and be free to fly without restrictions. It is about winds, a warm breeze, and a breeze which ruffles your hair. It gives you a feeling of freedom or releasing the fogginess of old thoughts. It is about the scents that are carried on the breeze; it is about the spark of lightning carried for miles. It is about feeling light and airy and having a lift to your step. When you need to lighten your mood or to carry a message of change, use a picture of clouds, a sound of the wind or waves being pushed by the winds crashing on the shore to give you a feeling of change or freedom.

Use your senses and the four elements to encourage a difference within your meditation and to create a renewed energy.

# Element Uses

The four elements we will be talking about are: air, earth, water and fire. These four elements can be included in a variety of ways.

**Air**: scents, a fan, breezes, a hand fan, wind chimes
**Fire**: candles, camp fire, fireplace, picture of fire
**Earth**: potted plants, sand in a bottle, container of sand with a little rake
**Water**: shower/bath, water in a bottle, drinking water, ocean/lake side, waterfall, pool side, rain, music with ocean sounds

There are traditional meanings for each of the elements and they are used symbolically in many ways.

**Air**: intellect and communication – intellectual – communicative, clever and fair – Gemini, Libra, Aquarius – being able to be above it all, releasing it up and away from you
**Fire**: spirit and energy – physical – self-sufficient, spontaneous and possessing a tremendous zest for life – Aries, Leo, Sagittarius – ritualistic burning off/total release, rising from the ashes
**Earth**: material things and security – practical – dependable and conservative – Taurus, Virgo, Capricorn – grounding yourself, coming back down to earth
**Water**: emotion and nurture – emotional – empathetic, receptive and feel things deeply – Cancer, Scorpio, Pisces – flowing with whatever is happening to you, allowing it to flow away from you

There is also an intermingling of the elements.

Earth with air – makes the earth softer and wind (air) can carry earth.

Earth with fire – earth can douse fire but fire can also burn off foliage so new growth can come.

Earth with water – earth with water can sustain growth and too much water is a flood but earth can hold water like a stream or ocean.

Air with fire – fire needs air to keep burning and you can stifle fire with a lack of air.

Air with water – air usually contains moisture and without air, water can be stagnant.

Fire with water – water can douse fire but fire can transform water into steam.

If you are going through a particular time or problem, you can use the elements to help you either to heal or project energy. Use them individually or in a combination.

# Element Meditations

S ome of the simplest ways to use the elements is to just walk in nature. It takes you on a journey of nature and makes you feel grounded and reconnected. Find and use the scavenger hunt items in the next section into your meditation circle. If you can't find the articles, use a picture or make a drawing of what you want to include.

## Seasons

**Fall**
This season is about harvesting and starting the new spiritual year. Use the fruits of this season – go to the farmers' markets and check out what is in harvest. Walk in the cool autumn air.

**Scavenger hunt**: pinecones, leaves, gourds, pumpkins, birch bark, chestnuts, seeds, acorns, stones, rose hips, twigs.

**Elements**: trees and pine cones (earth); frost (water); red leaves and sunsets (fire); autumn air (air).

**Winter**
This season is about hibernation and creation. Snow and ice are the more common seasonal elements. Walk in the snow and the frigid air.

**Scavenger hunt**: snow, ice, carrots and coal pieces for a snowman, mittens, fuzzy ear muffs, wool blankets, wood logs, candles, penguins.

**Elements**: bare trees (earth); snow (water); crackling fire (fire); cold air (air).

## Spring
This season is about rejuvenation and newness. Take a fresh walk in the spring sunshine.

**Scavenger hunt**: tulips, hyacinths, leaves, blossoms, robin's egg shell, feathers, Easter eggs.

**Elements**: Flowers, buds on trees (earth); spring runoff in streams (water); brighter sunshine (fire); fresh air (air).

## Summer
This season is all about fulfillment and fullness. Walk in the warm sunshine and along the warm water in the waterways.

**Scavenger hunt**: roses, strawberries, fruits, vegetables, tomatoes, suntan lotion, bug spray, lanterns, Adirondack chairs, hammocks.

**Elements**: grass and trees (earth); summer rain (water); lightning (fire); warm/hot breezes (air).

## <u>Holidays</u>

Celebrate your holidays in your meditations.

**Christmas**: tree (earth); icicles (water); candles and lights (fire); scents (air).
**New Year's Day**: calendar (earth); endings (water); fireworks (fire); resolutions (air).
**Valentine's Day**: heart shaped and chocolate (earth); emotions and love (water); red and pink (fire); cards and communication (air).
**Thanksgiving Day**: vegetables and fruits (earth); gratitude and harvesting (water); wine making (fire); beginning (air).

# Astrology and the Elements

In astrology, the four material elements relate to the signs: Fire, Earth, Air and Water. The astrological elements are expressions of spiritual energies, rather than blind forces. Use your own astrological sign to see how you fit in with these descriptions. Use the different quadrants below to accent your different meditations at specific times.

The astrological signs are:

**Fire signs**: Aries (Mar 21-Apr 19), Leo (Jul 23-Aug 22), Sagittarius (Nov 22-Dec 21)
**Earth signs**: Taurus (Apr 20-May 20), Virgo (Aug 23-Sept 22), Capricorn (Dec 22-Jan 19)
**Air signs**: Gemini (May 21-Jun 21), Libra (Sept 23-Oct 22), Aquarius (Jan 20-Feb 18)
**Water signs**: Cancer (Jun 22-Jul 22), Scorpio (Oct 23-Nov 21), Pisces (Feb 19-Mar 20)

The astrological signs also relate as elements and gender (Masculine = aggressive; Feminine = nurturing) are:

**Fire signs**: enthusiasm, inspiration, spirit (Masculine).
**Earth signs**: very practical, earthly, solid (Feminine).
**Air signs**: mental nature, gatherers of knowledge (Masculine).
**Water signs**: emotional nature, very reflective and sensitive (Feminine).

Each sign is also identified by its quality which is

**Cardinal** (creative): Aries, Cancer, Libra, Capricorn
**Fixed** (determined): Taurus, Leo, Scorpio, Aquarius

**Mutable** (changeable): Gemini, Virgo, Sagittarius, Pisces

**Elemental Compatibilities**

**Air**: Air signs work well with fire signs. Fire needs air to generate heat. The fire signs stimulate and help motivate the air signs into new ideas.
**Fire**: Compatible with air signs, fire signs encourage the ideas of the air signs. A fire sign takes your ideas and motivates and leads all to better sales and marketing while taking all the credit.
**Water**: Water signs work well with earth signs. Earth signs bring a need of stability and consistency to water that keeps it contained in a healthy calmer manner. Water signs dislike the strong boisterous personalities of the air and fire signs.
**Earth**: The fast moving, changeable air signs fascinate Earth signs. Fire signs are too forceful for their slower thorough nature. Earth signs share with the water signs the characteristics of retentiveness, self-protectiveness, and acquisitiveness. Water signs will soothe and comfort the earth people.

## Astrological Quadrants

View the astrological wheel in quadrants which corresponds to the seasons, like a pie cut into quarters. Each quadrant or quarter begins with a different element. It is not a coincidence that each of these quadrants coincides with the beginning of each season. Each quadrant begins with a different element. Therefore each season begins with a distinct energy.

A very brief review of the signs in order, with a brief descriptive:

**First Quadrant – Spring**
Aries - I am. (Fire) Taurus - I have. (Earth) Gemini - I think. (Air)
**Second Quadrant – Summer**
Cancer - I feel. (Water) Leo - I will. (Fire) Virgo - I analyze. (Earth)
**Third Quadrant – Fall**
Libra - I relate. (Air) Scorpio - I create. (Water) Sagittarius - I perceive. (Fire)
**Fourth Quadrant – Winter**
Capricorn - I use. (Earth) Aquarius - I know. (Air) Pisces - I believe. (Water)

# Astrology Meditations

Astrology and the different aspects are very interesting to use in your meditations. There is a whole belief system around the signs and their elements and what everything means. You can examine them more but for now we will use simple ways to incorporate them into your meditations. If you don't know someone's sign, try to guess what their sign/element is. The oldest line in a bar is "What's your sign?" Rather than going to a bar, just watch people and be aware of what is going on. Even our animals have astrological signs – see if they are true to their signs.

**Meditations:**

1. Focus on your astrological sign/element and the sign/element that is in play at the present time. Create a meditation around the two signs/elements highlighting both qualities and how they interact.
2. Focus on your astrological sign/element and your family and friends who surround you. Check out what elements are combined with all of you and how many are similar. Be aware of your interactions.
3. Focus on your astrological sign/element and the people who you work with if you know their sign. Check out what elements are combined with all of you and how many are similar. Be aware of your interactions.
4. Focus on your astrological sign/element and the people who you don't get along with if you know their sign. Be aware of your interactions.

# Numbers

# Numbers and Their Meanings

Numbers are very effective to use when you choose your options for your meditations. It is easier to use a number then to just "wing" what you are doing. When first teaching a class, I always use the number "3" or a combination of "3" such as six or nine for the class – three breaths, three times, or three repetitions. This way there is less confusion when I give them something to do. When you have a theme, add repeat prayers, and/or instructions to emphasize your theme. When you are including items, use a number of items to signify what you are meditating on.

As you can see, the numbers are from one to nine. All numbers can be reduced to a single digit simply by adding the numbers together. You can take your birth date and add all the numbers together and reduce it to one number. You can do this with your address or any number you are associated with.

**One:** strong will, pure energy, new beginnings, physical and mental energies, natural forces, take action, and start a new venture.

**Two:** kindness, balance, tact, equalization, and duality, the need for planning, choices, exchanges made with others, partnerships (both in harmony and rivalry), and communication, uniting with like-minds, and like-ideals, natural flow of judgment.

**Three:** magic, intuition, expression, versatility, and pure joy and expression of creativity, identifier as it represents past, present and future, or consider your present directional path in relation to past events and future goals, promising new adventures, reward and success in most undertakings.

**Four:** stability and invokes the grounded nature of all things, the four seasons, four directions, four elements, solidity, calmness, and home, need to get back to your roots, center yourself, or even "plant" yourself, persistence and endurance.

**Five:** travel, adventure, motion, instability, unpredictability, radical changes, wild vibrations, primitive and erratic, prepare for some action, like a trip in the mind and spirit.

**Six:** harmony, balance, sincerity, love, and truth, reveals solutions for us in a calm, unfolding manner, enlightenment.

**Seven:**_magical forces, esoteric, aspects of magic, scholarly activities, mystery, impractical dreaming.

**Eight:** business, success, and wealth, continuation, repetition, and cycles, elements in success, because of dogged determination and repetition, and growing momentum.

**Nine:** vibration frequencies, attainment, satisfaction, accomplishment, success, intellectual power, inventiveness, recognition of our own internal attributes.

# Cards and Their Meanings

When I have classes, one is always about "Being Psychic" and I bring in a series of cards which include tarot cards. I always enjoy seeing my class wonder why I am doing that class but it is to show that everything has a value including different cards. There have been many people who have beautiful ideas and they either write a book or make a set of cards. So the class practices with the cards and the mystery is gone because they understand their purpose. They have a totally different idea about them. Most never buy a deck of cards but that is totally alright.

Regular or Tarot cards can add a dimension to your meditations. There are many card sets that you can use. Tarot cards come in different themes with their own descriptions and there are numerous decks available. If you are using cards, pick one that is gentle you enjoy the illustrations which will help you understand the cards.

There are cards which just have positive sayings, affirmations and wordings on them and are simple to use. Many card sets have spiritual meanings to them like angel cards but still pick what is compatible to you. Check the pictures on the cards and the card meanings to see if they are suited to you. They are relatively inexpensive. Have fun with it.

Below are the different descriptions of the suits used in card sets. If you use a spread, pay attention to what suit comes up more often or use that specific suit for your meditation.

**Diamonds:** The Mind, practical and material matters
Season: Spring
Tarot: Pentacles, Coins, Disks, Stones
Element: Earth and Air

Astrology: Taurus, Virgo, Capricorn
Direction: north, midnight
Area of concern: Material wealth, money, practicality, logical, material plane, physical body and health

**Clubs:** Foundations, power of transmutation
Season: Summer
Tarot: Wands, Rods, Batons, Staves
Element: Fire and Water
Astrology: Aries, Leo, Sagittarius
Direction: south, noonday
Area of concern: Energy, growth, enterprise, success, spiritual impulse and creative energy

**Hearts:** Being in rhythm, the emotions, intuition, psychic faculties
Season: Autumn
Tarot: Cups, Chalices
Element: Water and Fire
Astrology: Cancer, Scorpio, Pisces
Direction: west, twilight
Area of concern: Emotions, love, beauty, compassionate, growth of the spirit, balancing the emotions and nurturing the spirit

**Spades:** Growth and wisdom, power of the mind
Season: Winter
Direction: east, sunrise
Tarot: Swords
Element: Air and Earth
Astrology: Gemini, Libra, Aquarius
Area of concern: Intellect, courage, aggression, strength, mental qualities and attributes

**Card Meanings:**

Ace or One: New beginnings, opportunity
Two: Balance, choices, crossroads, duality
Three: Growth, achievement, expression
Four: Containment, structure, stability, stagnation

Five: Minor conflict, uncertainties, instability, loss, opportunity for change
Six: Formation of certainties, communication, problem-solving, cooperation
Seven: Achievement, abilities developed, reflection, assessment, motives
Eight: Movement towards goal, action, change, power
Nine: Culmination, reckoning, fruition, attainment
Ten: Completion, end of cycle
Joker (male or female): Something unexpected and/or uncontrolled can occur
Queen: Fertility, creativity, mysteries, hidden meanings
King: Authority, leadership, spiritual guidance, choosing a solitary path, finding a teacher

Meditations:

See above for the meanings and the elements related to the different suits. Some suggested uses for cards can be:

1. Pull a card and look at the above meanings or read your cards' accompanying book to see the significance. Meditate on its meaning.
2. Ask a question which is on your mind and then pull 1or more cards and place them in front of you. Check out the significance and meditate on it.
3. Clear your mind and pull three cards. The first represents your past, second is your present and the third is your future. Meditate on the meanings.

# Lucky Bamboo Stalks

B amboo stalks represent Chinese symbols of good luck. Lucky Bamboo signifies good fortune, health and prosperity. It can easily be bought at local stores, flower or garden shops and is very inexpensive.

Lucky Bamboo activates stagnant energy and enhances the flow of positive energy, or auspicious chi (energy), throughout your home or workplace. It is important to take proper care of your Lucky Bamboo ensuring its health and vitality.

These easy to grow plants require very little care and are generally grown in water or hydroponically. To care for Lucky Bamboo you need the following:

A container
Small stones or pebbles
A solution of diluted plant food
Indirect light.

In Feng Shui, a Bamboo plant usually has a combination of all the Chinese five elements which include:

Wood: The bamboo plant
Earth: The stones or pebbles
Metal: The container itself (if it is made of glass, use a small metal figure or coin attached to the container)
Water: The water in which the Lucky Bamboo plant grows
Fire: A red ribbon tied around the bamboo stalks or the container itself.

# Number of Stalks

**One stalk:** A meaningful and simple life and overall good fortune.

**2 stalks:** Happy relationships, luck in love and double luck.

**3 stalks:** Happiness, wealth and longevity. Towers - better, promotions, more of the good things of life, climbing.

**3 stalks with a curly stalk in the middle**: Wealth (the curly stalk signifies money).

**4 stalks**: Creativity and successful academic achievement and good luck with love.

**5 stalks:** five Chinese elements of life representing wealth - Represents a balance of good luck in all aspects of life, happiness.

**6 stalks:** Luck in Chinese, a flow of good luck, easy money, wealth and prosperity, favorable conditions.

**7 stalks:** Good luck in relationships; good health.

**8 stalks:** Fertility and good luck to thrive and grow.

**9 stalks:** Overall good health, prosperity and a successful love life.

**10 stalks:** A complete and fulfilling life.

**11 stalks:** General good luck in all aspects of life.

**21 stalks:** All-purpose powerful blessing.

# Time & Directions

# Time Captured

C an we capture time? There are sixty seconds to a minute; sixty minutes to an hour; twenty-four hours in a day; seven days in a week; fifty-two weeks in a year; twelve months in a year. Then we break it down to three months in a season; four seasons in a year to the earth cycle. The moon has a monthly lunar cycle and the sun has a yearly solar cycle.

There are holidays both spiritual, personal and community based like Labour Day and Thanksgiving. We celebrate times of the year, seasons or personal aspects like births, communions, marriages, or graduations.

In all, there are continuous cycles. These can be used in your meditations. In a cycle, there is a beginning, middle and an end. It is like everything else in our lives. It begins and ends only to begin again renewed.

Take time to celebrate each part. Celebrate the beginnings, renewals and inner creations – the innocent times. Celebrate the middle, the blossoming, the conjunct of all things; the apex that time flows around. Celebrate the endings, the culmination, the completion, and the outer as it disperses outward. Then welcome the new as you open up to new possibilities.

Time flows whether we want it to or not. To capture it is to attempt to stop its movement. All things end so learn to accept the inevitable and use it. Journal at the hardest times and then those times will also begin again in innocence. At times when it seems the darkest begins the dawn of a new day – time flows.

# Portions of Time

The time of the day, month, season can all be used to add dimension to your meditations. These are suggested examples which can be used.

**Moon cycles**: Full (culmination, fullness), Waning (ending, banish negativity), New (beginning), Waxing (preparations, growing in power).

**Day**: Sunrise (banish leftover negativity), late morning (strength, efficiency, guidance and energy), sunset (willpower, calmness, serenity, newness), night (psychic energy, reflection, re-plan).

**Days**: Sunday (leadership and health), Monday (fertility and growth), Tuesday (competition and finances), Wednesday (self-expression and wisdom), Thursday (health and wealth), Friday (faith and trust), Saturday (fidelity).

**Months**: January (future plans), February (assist in challenges), March (encouragement), April (fertilization), May (sprouting), June (love and employment), July (increase prosperity), August (full term), September (harvesting), October (abundance), November (strengthen bonds), December (sweeping out old and preparation for new).

**Seasons**: Fall (harvesting and beginning the yearly plan), Winter (hibernating and creating), Spring (coming to life/sprouting), Summer (fullness, ripening).

**Meditations:**

1. Pick a theme and incorporate the time of day, moon cycle or season into it. Sit with your theme and the time of year.

2. Fall is the time to write down your wishes for the coming year. Write down your wishes, date them and seal them till next fall. Open your list up next fall and see how many have come true or are in process and update them or add another part to them. Add more wishes for the next fall, date the additions and seal it. Repeat the opening of your list every year.

3. At times, it is enough just to sit in the moonlight or lack of it. Open your curtains up and sit and let the moon flow down on you. Sit quietly and let it envelop you. Enjoy.

# Directions and Belief Systems

There are some different types of beliefs listed below. Each represents a belief system which is inherent to them. As you can see in each of them, each direction has strength and quality and is representative of other elements. If there is one belief system that draws you to it, then search it out on the internet. It might have slightly different variations on this theme but use the strength and power that is in their perception of qualities. This is all about finding direction and guidance within your meditations. Use and enjoy what these bring you.

*C = color; S = season; E = element*

## Native Indian Spirituality

**West** *(C = black; S = autumn)*
Animal: Thunder Beings
Stage of Life: Infancy
Human Value: Sharing and Generosity
Represents: death, personal truths and inner answers, the path to your goals
Denotes: final harvest, the end of Life's Cycle

**North** *(C = red, blue; S = winter)*
Animal: Buffalo
Stage of Life: Youth
Human Value: Internal strength and fortitude
Represents: sadness, defeat, wise counsel and teaches us when to speak and when to listen
Denotes: survival and waiting

**East** *(C = yellow, red; S = spring)*
Animal: Elk
Stage of Life: Adulthood
Human Value: Respect for Traditions
Represents: victory, power, greatest spiritual challenges and illumination
Denotes: re-awakening after a long sleep, victory over winter; the power of new life.

**South** *(C = white; S = summer)*
Animal: Owl
Stage of Life: Elder
Human Value: Wisdom
Represents: peace, happiness and serenity, the inner child, when to be humble and trust, innocence
Denotes: time of plenty

**Up Above** *(C = yellow)*
Association: Sky, Great Spirit
Represents: guardian of your dream time, personal access to other dimensions

**Here in the Center** *(C = green)*
Association: Mother, Nourishment

**Below**
Association: inner earth
Represents: how to stay grounded and on the path

**Within**
Association: protector of your sacred space
Represents: your heart's joy and faithfulness to personal truths

**Right Side**
Association: Father-protector within
Represents: male side protection and carries your courage and warrior spirit

**Left Side**
Association: female side protector
Represents: receiving abundance and nurturing yourself and others, your teacher about relationships and mothering.

## Chinese Tradition and Feng Shui

**East (*C = blue, green; S = spring; E = wood*)**
Time of Day: Morning
Represents: Leadership, assertiveness, creativity, planning, decision-making, competitiveness, conflict, anger, frustration.
Denotes: Wind
Energy: growth and vitality

**South (*C = red; S = summer; E = fire*)**
Time of Day: Mid-day
Represents: Self-expression, emotional extremes, empathy, extrovert, attention-seeking, sociable, talkative
Denotes: Heat
Energy: strongest in summer, early June, and at noon time

**West (*C = white; S = autumn; E = metal*)**
Time of Day: Evening
Represents: Precise, meticulous, logical, analytical, moderation, self-control, morality, tendency for pessimism
Denotes: Dryness
Energy: condensing and contracting the earth

**North (*C = black; S = winter; E = water*)**
Time of Day: Night
Represents: Solitude, privacy, introspection, philosophy, mystery, truth, honesty, anxiety, nervousness, insecurity
Denotes: Cold
Energy: resting and stillness

**Center (***C = yellow; S =late summer; E = earth***)**
Time of Day: Afternoon
Represents: Caring, supportive, nourishing, family-oriented, stability, grounding, "mother hen", worrier
Denotes: Dampness
Energy: grounding, stabilizing and balancing

## Wicca (white) Witch religion (used as parts of a sacred space/circle)

**East (***E = air***)**
Represents: intellect, awareness and creativity

**South (***E = fire***)**
Represents: personal power, innocence and trust

**West (***E = water***)**
Represents: dreams, introspection and emotions

**North (***E = earth***)**
Represents: wisdom, ritual, learning and rituals

**Meditations:**

1. Pick a belief system and direction. Sit quietly and allow yourself to feel the quality which it represents. You don't have to believe it but just allow the perception to flow through you.
2. Instinctively we look in a direction when we are quiet. I love to see the sunset so it seems my direction is the west. Be aware of what is natural for you.
3. When you are having problems and can't seem to focus, honor each direction and then sit comfortably and let your soul choose. Don't fight it but let it guide you.

# Vibrations

# Colors and Their Meanings

Colors are very beneficial to add to your meditations or to your regular life. Be aware of how you feel when you add a different color. Use the included list of color meanings to give you a suggested guidance. Be aware if you feel the same or different.

Colors can be added in:

1. Clothes
2. Mats, cushions, draping cloths
3. Trinkets, pictures, different magazine pictures
4. Flowers (real or silk)
5. Crystals, candles
6. Colored light bulbs
7. Computer screen savers
8. Painting your walls or sections
9. Drinks – orange, cranberry, lemonade, etc.

**Black:** protection of oneself or others; a hidden or understood ability that needs to come forth, opens deeper levels of unconsciousness to induce deep meditational state, banish evil or negativity.

**Blue (light):** spiritual color, peace and tranquility to home, synthesizing.

**Blue (Royal):** dreams, sensations, sixth sense, clairvoyance, intuition, mysticism, promotes laughter and joviality, loyalty, increased influence, energy of night.

**Blue:** compassion, understanding, contemplation, wisdom, aspirations, protection, speech, hearing, harmony, inner light or peace, confers truth and guidance.

**Brown:** earthy and earth-bound, a connection to nature or natural processes, physically oriented, practical, balanced color, financial success, improves powers of concentration, study, telepathy.

**Clear:** energy of all colors, combination of all, perfect balance and harmony, clarity, crystal clear, solidification, reflection, recognition, paradox, invisible, subconscious, intensity, timeless, natural, classic, quality, quiet, full moon.

**Coral:** energy of continual rhythm, cleansing, life's boundary, protection.

**Gold:** color of universal love, spiritual rewards, refinement, strengthens all fields of the body and spirit, energy of newness, wisdom, stability, luck or money, solar energy.

**Green (emerald):** attracts love, social delights and fertility.

**Green (olive):** energy of newness, regeneration, restoration, stamina, endurance, strength, permanence, trust.

**Green:** healing skills, hope, peace, serenity, energy of the heart, sustenance, love freely given, fertility, success, good luck, harmony, rejuvenation.

**Grey:** pondering complex issues in meditation, magic, sparks confusion, negates or neutralizes negative influence.

**Indigo:** color of inertia, stops situations or people, used for deeper meditations.

**Lavender:** equilibrium, spiritual healing.

**Magenta (red/violet):** energy of promise, beginnings, energizing, profound healing, energizes rituals for immediate action.

**Orange:** Creativity, energy of vitality, balance, equilibrium, gut feelings/ wisdom, ability to speak one's mind, ambition, career matters, self-confidence, solar energy.

**Pink:** color of human love: combines white of spirit/purpose with red which protects/provides life, joy, affection, kindness, new life, in the moment, femininity, honor, service.

**Purple:** deeply intuitive, color of transformation, devotion, healing abilities, compassion, power, success, idealism, independence.

**Red:** life, passion, energy, optimism, fighting instinct, earth connection, survival, health, fertility, strength, courage, will power, magnetism.

**Silver:** transmission, justice and purity, excellent protective energies, peace and persistence, removes negativity, encourages stability, develops psychic abilities.

**Turquoise (Blue/yellow):** energy of feeling, intuition, emotions, communication, teaching, healing.

**Violet:** energy of ritual, magic, mystery, letting go, rejuvenation, completion, renewal, spirituality, deep healing, fall.

**White:** relates to principles, concepts and purpose, purity, perfection, holiness, balance of all colors, spiritual enlightenment, cleansing, clairvoyance, healing, truth seeking, lunar energy.

**Yellow:** intellectual, mental, renewal, life energy, practical thought, inspiration, vibrancy, optimism, activity, solar energy, energy of sunshine.

# Candles and Ambiance

C andles are so common and yet they give such an ambience to our meditations and our regular lives. They were here long before we used hydro to light our lives. Practice your meditations with their subdued light and use this as a quiet time to embrace the semi-darkness.

Uses and benefits:

1. Light is the very sustenance of spiritual and earthly life.
2. The flame provides both heat and warmth.
3. Ambience is added to your gatherings or events.
4. Scented, brightly colored candles can be used as a special centerpiece on altars or holiday tables.
5. The flickering light of a candle flame can help raise spiritual energy in rituals, ceremonies, prayers or meditations. It can help bring a sense of calm and peace.
6. The lighting of candles represents joy and is a common ritual for local community events.
7. A candle can be lit at your personal altar to celebrate a personal joy, for prayers or share concerns.
8. For various purposes such as a healing or a protection ritual, light a candle to absorb negative energies and then release it with the flame of the candle.
9. During meditations it can help to create an atmosphere of peace or as a visual focal point.
10. It can symbolize spirit, divinity, truth, devotion or a way in which one can connect with a higher power.

# Meditating and Visualizing
## with Colored Candles

Candles can be used to enhance meditation and well-being in the areas associated with their color. This is particularly true while practicing visualizations. You can use colors to bring positive aspects into your life. Each color is shown along with a suggested symbology. If you are unable to get colored candles, a colored holder for the candle can be used so the light coming through is colored.

**Black:** Protection from physical harm; completion e.g. such as a relationship, death of a loved one; believed to stop negative thoughts and remove confusion.

**Blue:** Used to concentrate on health, self-expression, peace and tranquility.

**Brown:** Serenity, peace, earthy.

**Green:** Prosperity, money, and attracting wealth; marriage, good fortune or getting pregnant.

**Indigo:** Electric in nature, intuition, spirituality; color of power.

**Light and dark colors:** Color with black added brings a darker shade and both the protection of black with the color symbolism. Color with white added brings with it both the color symbolism and the white purity and protection from corruption.

**Orange:** Visualization; stimulating color related to healing energies; healing for sudden losses or changes.

**Pink:** Love, friendship, happiness.

**Pink (Dark):** Finding a pure, gentle, unconditional love; concentrating on spiritual healing.

**Pink (Light):** Emotions of love, romance, and a true shared spiritual awakening.

**Purple:** psychic powers; comfort; dignity, spirituality, and success; vibrancy to attract people.

**Red:** Pure energy, creative and physical; releases passion, power, sexuality.

**White:** For higher awareness, protection (on the material plane); centering yourself; inner peace, spirituality, and attaining a higher power.

**Yellow:** Visualize greater intellect and will; concentrating on creative endeavors; increasing psychic awareness and clairvoyance; expanding your imagination.

# The Power of Scents

An important sensory tool to use to change the atmosphere of your home is scent. Whenever you enter someone's home you're usually aware of their particular scent. With incense, fragrant oils or candles you can influence your personal signature to create perhaps the strongest of all impressions, fragrance.

Scents tell us much more than we're aware of and are why the power of scent should not be underestimated. Here are some ways scents can change us:

- Our scent receptors are closely linked to the emotional centers of the brain and can therefore trigger strong emotions. Smells can trigger specific memories and emotions from as early as childhood. Each person perceives smells differently, depending on their earlier experiences. Men respond differently to scents than women.
- The different sensory cells in your nose detect smells you inhale, each reacting to only certain components in a smell. The inability to smell certain scents is quite common.
- People who have lost their sense of smell because of accidental injury or illness frequently report a sudden loss in sexual drive and reduced sexual pleasure. In general their emotions are "blunted", meaning that their highs and lows are not as extreme as those of individuals with an intact sense of smell. The variety of emotions that they show also seems limited and may often be depressed and lethargic.
- Scents are involved in social interactions and almost all living things depend on the sense of smell for their existence. It has also been associated with instincts and the basic needs of survival, nutrition and mating.

- Smell memory holds all aspects of a moment remembered: sounds, sights, faces and thoughts. It can even affect our learning process
- Sense of smell helps us to avoid dangers, such as fire or rotten food.

Over the last two or more decades, there has been renewed interest in the therapeutic powers of plant scents and essences. Aromatherapy is the use of aromatic plant oils to promote health and well-being. Today, there are countless shops and boutiques selling aromatherapy products designed to relax, revive, calm and soothe. Below are some of the more popular ones.

**Cinnamon**: Smelling cinnamon can boost brain functions, performance and memory. Smelling cinnamon actually can enhance multiple areas of brain processing and function from memory to visual-motor speed to recognition to attention and focus.

**Eucalyptus:** It has a powerful scent and is easily recognizable. It is used as an antiseptic, antispasmodic, decongestant, diuretic and stimulant. It also has cooling properties, which gives it deodorizing characteristics. This cooling capability also helps with muscle aches and pains. It can help fight migraines and fevers.

**Jasmine:** A voluptuous yet subtle scent, it is famous for its ability to heal a woman's sense of herself, restoring self-esteem, renewing a feeling of attractiveness, reducing tension and stress.

**Lavender:** Lavender is one of the most popular essential oils. In addition to stress-relieving properties, lavender is a healing aid against colds, flu and migraines.

**Lemon:** Lemon is widely appreciated for its "clean" smell, but has numerous therapeutic qualities as well. It improves concentration, aids in digestion and eases symptoms of acne and arthritis.

**Peppermint**: Peppermint has a cooling, refreshing effect and is widely used to enhance mental alertness. It is a cooling agent that enhances mood, sharpens focus, combats irritation and redness, alleviates symptoms of congestion, and aids in digestion.

**Rose:** a powerful aromatherapy treatment for issues related to females. It helps with a number of illnesses and conditions, such as depression, anxiety and digestion issues. It also helps with circulation, heart problems and respiratory conditions like asthma. It is a protector of the heart.

**Rosemary:** Rosemary is a wonderful mental stimulant. It enhances memory, relieves congestion and sinusitis issues.

**Sandalwood:** Sandalwood is easily recognized by its woody fragrance. It is used as a relaxing agent for tension relief, for its energizing qualities and aphrodisiac effects.

**Vanilla:** Vanilla's sugary sweet aroma has been known to assist in curing ailments. It relaxes the spirit and has associations of comfort and satisfaction, gentle relaxation, and sensuality.

**Ylang-Ylang:** Its sweet aroma is excellent for reducing stress and as an aphrodisiac. Used properly it stimulates sensuality, soothe headaches and is an anti-depressant.

One way to set the mood in your room is to use scented candles. It can turn an ordinary room into a magical setting for romance or meditation. There are various scented candles that can be used for romance, prosperity and spiritual growth. Choose the color and scents that symbolize your intentions and use a fire-safe holder.

Incense is another way to bring scent into your environment. Incense can be quite strong so use with caution and with the proper holder to collect the ashes as the incense burns.

These are all some inexpensive ways to create an environment that symbolizes and energizes your desires.

**Meditations:**

1. In a spritzer bottle add filtered water then add some of your favorite scented oils. Spray it around then smell the air. Feel what memories or emotions the scent(s) stirs within you.

2. Use incense, scented candles, spices, cedar wood pieces, flowers, fresh herbs, scented oils or creams, aromatic foods, perfumes, etc. Take your time and enjoy the scents which surround you. Be aware of how they make you feel.

3. Take a walk in nature and use your sense of smell to feel the natural scents which surround you. Stop and close your eyes and be aware of the smell of grass, trees, pine needles, green growth, flowers and everything else in your surroundings.

# Music of the Soul

Music has the power to

1.  heal wounds of the mind and heart,
2.  relieve stress,
3.  lift the spirit, and
4.  ease emotional burdens.

Our sense of hearing is affected on many levels because it detects every sound as vibrations and frequencies which create internal and external vibrational waves. It creates a change in our energy either good or bad. It can create a soothing effect like a silk scarf being stroked across our body or a grating on our nerves and the hair on our body lifting. At other times, we ignore it completely because we are always surrounded by sound. Even if the music grates on our nerves, it stimulates us to feel something. Music can be a simple thing that can be extremely effective.

The sounds which surround us can alter our mood or change our daily experience. One simple solution to a very hectic day is to turn on a favorite music CD, and as you listen to the music you find your tense muscles unclench, your shoulders relax and lower, your heart rate slows and returns to normal.

Music allows our spirit to soar. When a piece of music touches you, some indefinable part of your consciousness ascends to new heights.

Pay attention to the music you listen to in the different times of your life. What music draws you and which changes how you feel? Use different music to create feelings. Know what rocks your world and what brings peace. Be aware of the different musical instruments and the sounds that create a difference in how you feel. What makes your feet automatically start to dance? Use that and dance barefoot to it!!! What makes you automatically start to sing? Find what does that for you and sing at the top of your lungs. What makes your hips move or shoulders rock? Every one of us has those tunes which make us forget ourselves and shake our hips or want to dance barefoot. Do it and do it often. That feeling will stay with you long after the music ends.

A suggested guide to use to induce different feelings is below. Find recordings with these types of music to help you feel differently. Experiment with different sounds through your library and find what appeals to you. Use them in your meditations.

**Earthy music (grounding):** Deep-low drums, Bassoon, Primitive drum rolls.

**Creating (opening up):** Electric guitar, Marimbas, Saxophone.

**Power (inner/strengthening):** Cello, Violin, Oboe, Piano, Guitar.

**Heart (healing/expanding):** Harp, Flute, Violin, Piano.

**Speaking truth:** the Human Voice, Flute, Woodwinds.

**Seeing beyond your present circumstances:** higher electronic instruments and synthesizers.

**Higher spiritual energy:** organ, electronic instruments and sounds.

# Crystals, Gems
# and Metals

# Crystal Uses

Crystals have been used since the time of the Continent of Atlantis to light their cities. They were also used in numerous ways similar to electricity by the American and Australian Indigenous nations for their religious ceremonies and healing. Crystals were used in Egypt thousands of years ago and also mentioned in the Bible. The use of crystals is not a modern theory but a form of energy emission that has been known for centuries and used for healing the body.

Crystals are referred to as the gifts from the earth and help keep us grounded and closer to nature. Crystals are stronger in their natural rough state with very little changes or modifications.

The human body is made of energy and crystals emit different vibrations which affect the energy flow.

**Choosing Crystals:**

1. Clearly identify your purpose in having the crystal
2. Consult books and the internet to find what crystal(s) would support you in your purpose
3. Pick a sample which offers the vibration you need
4. Hold the crystal in your hand or think of holding it in your hand and state your purpose in a positive way
5. Feel the response (falling forward is good – feeling of going backward and away isn't good)
6. Make a conscious decision to accept the influence
7. Place your crystal beside a small water fountain of some kind to maximize its strength

Crystals are very powerful to use within a meditation. It can increase or calm your energy. There is a wide variety of crystals and a multitude of benefits from them. If you are confused about which one to try, start with a quartz (clear, rose, amethyst) and then check out some others.

Cleanse your crystals (see below) when you buy them and use them often.

**Meditations:**

1.  While meditating, hold them in your hand(s).
2.  Circle yourself with them especially in the north, south, west and east directions and sit facing the direction you feel comfortable with. Initially do this for short periods at a time.
3.  Keep them in your home and/or office area to keep your energy on them.
4.  Wear them as jewelry. You can buy stones and little cages to hold them and then hang them on a chain of your choice.
5.  Lay with them along the center of your body and in your hands.
6.  Bathe with them in your water or in the shower.
7.  Place them under your pillow or mattress.
8.  Keep them in your pocket or on a key chain.

# Crystals Cleansing

S ome types of crystal will come in the form of a clear, pointed stone. Other crystals may be smooth but use what feels right for you. Crystals vary in size, shape, clarity, color, textures, and purity. Size doesn't matter although you might consider the size for the purpose you are using it for. If you are carrying it around with you, find one that fits well in your purse or pocket. If you are carrying a small pouch with several crystals, then consider smaller versions of crystals. At times, just having crystals around is enough. Use your feelings to select individual crystals or clusters so they will add sparkle and balance to your home or environment.

Use a prayer, affirmation or mantra when programming your crystal to emit the energy and use of your stone. If you don't have one then use the affirmation e.g. "I am happy."

Sometimes a stone or crystal you are strongly drawn to originally or that felt good previously doesn't feel the same now. This is understandable that you have changed so your taste in crystals has changed. In other cases, the stone or crystal may need to be cleared/cleansed. The clearer the energy of a stone, the more powerful it is. Crystals and healing gemstones need to be cleared as soon as they are purchased as well as clearing after every sustained use. A cleared, ready crystal feels positive, bright, tingly and cold to the touch. A crystal that needs clearing may feel hot, heavy or drained. There are a number of ways to effectively clear crystals and gemstones.

By rotating through these various clearing techniques, you will give your crystals a little edge and improve their performance in meditation. Each of these clearing methods will leave your crystals with a different feel and handling ability. Also ask the store you are buying your crystals from for suggesting on cleansing.

# Cleansing

**Cedar or Sage smudging or incense sticks:** Smudging is an excellent way to make sure your stones are purified. Pass your stone through the smoke of burning sage, incense or cedar sticks.

**Dried herbs:** Burying your crystal in a cupful of dried herbs will clear it. Suggested herbs for this are rose petals, sage, frankincense, myrrh, and sandalwood. You can usually find these at low cost at many co-ops or herb stores. This is a gentle and pleasant way to clear crystals, but it does take longer.

**Earth buried:** Crystals can also be buried in the earth. Outdoors, simply dig a hole the size of your crystal, place your crystal in the hole and cover with soil. The amount of time needed is a personal choice. Be sure to mark the spot with perhaps a stick or some other marker. You can also use a flower pot to bury your stone in. In the morning, carefully unearth the stones and wash them off with water. The ground method will enable the earth to absorb large amounts of negativity rapidly. This rapid absorption of negative energy can be an advantage when surrounded with an excess of negatively focused people, ideas, or you suffer from depression.

**Moonlight:** Place your crystals outside from the Full to the New Moon. Waning Moons are good times to clear crystals, to dispel old energies, but any time works. The amount of time used varies with how much the stone needs cleansing.

**Nature/Rain/thunderstorms:** Lay them out in the rain (negative ions!), especially during thundershowers. Place in water from the ocean or a sacred spring, or take it to a mountain or a grove of very old trees.

**Other types of crystals:** Your crystal will be enhanced by placing them on a crystal cluster or under a pyramid.

**Sea Salt:** Sea salt is the most traditional way for the initial cleansing. Salt can be mixed with water or used dry. To use salt water, mix a tablespoon of sea salt in a glass or ceramic cup of cold water. Do not use plastic or metal containers. Place the stones in the solution and allow to soak overnight. To use dry salt, place sea salt in a glass or non-plastic container and bury the crystals in the salt. Again, leave overnight. For those who live by the ocean, salt water can be used in a jar or gently wash them directly in the ocean.

*When clearing gemstone necklaces it is best to use the dry sea salt method. Be sure to use sea salt only, table salt contains aluminum and other chemicals.*

**Sunlight:** Expose your crystals to natural energy. Caution is required if there are internal fractures in your crystals which may cause your stone to crack or break if placed in direct hot sunlight. Put them out in sunlight for 24 hours.

**Tap water:** Run them under cool tap water. Make sure the points are facing down the drain to run the negative energy right down the sink. Never use warm or hot water, this could possibly fracture or break your crystals. Visualize the crystal as sparkly, tingly, and cold. For a quick, temporary cleaning, rinse it in cold water while imagining white or gold light running through the crystal, bottom to tip and out.

**Water fountain proximity:** Place your crystal close to a small water fountain. Do not place them in the water, as the mineral deposits might damage them so close to anywhere near the fountain will do. This allows the water energy to disperse the negative vibrations.

# Crystals, Gems and Metals

*H = healing; P = protection; S = strength; C = courage; L = luck;* ♥ *= love*

**Agate:** *H, P, S C,* ♥ longevity, gardening.

**Amber:** *H, P, S, L,* ♥ allows body to heal itself, stimulates intellect, cleanses environment, purify mind, beauty.

**Amethyst:** *H, P,* ♥ enhances intuitive and psychic abilities as well as visualization. Calming, strong protective abilities; reduces negative energies; helps to transform anger, nightmares, and irritability, dreams, peace.

**Apache Tear:** *P, L,* good-luck charm.

**Aquamarine:** *L, C,* positive energy, creativity, joy and flexibility. Reduces fear, angst and a lack of harmony, enhances connection. Peace and purification.

**Bloodstone:** *H, S, C,* ♥, an intense healing stone for purification. Revives love and relationships, victory, wealth, agriculture.

**Carnelian:** *H, P, C,* helps with issues of survival, energy and sexuality. Benefits include increased drive and confidence. Strengthens creativity, speech, peace, eloquence.

**Citrine:** material gain, business success and prosperity, clarity in thought and emotions, self-discipline. Enhances healing abilities, raises self-esteem, light heartedness, cheerfulness, hope, energizing, attracts abundance.

**Copper:** combats lethargy, passivity and non-acceptance of self.

**Coral:** *H, P,* corresponds to heart and internal systems of the body. It increases both physical and emotional strength, peace, wisdom.

**Diamond:** *P, S, C,* hardest of minerals, magnifies emotional states both positive and negative. Dispels negativity, abundance, innocence, purity, peace, reconciliation, and faithfulness.

**Emerald:** *P* ♥, more costly than a diamond, resonates with heart chakra, love, devotion and emotional balance, useful to dispel depression, money, mental powers, eyesight.

**Fluorite:** mental clarity, conscious mind, gaining perspective, analytical abilities, theorizing, quells strong emotions, smoothes over anger, desperation, depression or anger.

**Garnet** – *P, S,*♥, strengthens and purifies, vitalizes and regenerates, enhances creativity and imagination, compassion, endurance and vigor.

**Gold:** amplifies thought forms, purifies and energizes physical body, improves circulation and strengthens nervous system.

**Hematite:** *H,* the most grounding of all stones, calming, soothing, stabilizing, aids in sleeping.

**Jade:** *C,* highly prized in Asia, encourages compassion, emotional balance and generosity. Increases longevity, clarity, justice, wisdom, prosperity, dispels negativity, humility.

**Jasper:** *H, P, C,* chronic health issues or low energy, health, and beauty, mental processes, relieves pain, luck.

**Lapis Lazuli:** *H, P, C,*♥, reduces anxiety, restlessness, symbolizes spirituality, developing intuition. Promotes clarity, objectivity, detachment and wisdom. Augments vitality and virility. Improves communication and creative expression, soothing, gentleness, joy, fidelity.

*Elizabeth Banfalvi*

**Malachite:** *P,♥,* increase clairvoyance and concentration. Useful for the release of inflammation, irritation and depression. Aids sleep, emotional balancer. Reduces anger, and promotes peace, business success, tranquility.

**Moonstone:** *P,♥,* maintains and enhances female health, sleep, gardening, dieting.

**Moss Agate:** promotes agreeability, persuasiveness and negotiation strength.

**Obsidian:** *P,* grounding, centering, peace.

**Onyx:** *P,* helps relieve stress, balances male/female polarities, aids detachment, gives greater self-control and self-confidence, grounding, defensive magic.

**Opal:** *L,* happy dreams and changes, creativity, releases inhibitions, strengthens memory, intuition, inner beauty, money, power.

**Pearl:** *P, L,* increases patience, peace, reduces over sensitivity. Loving vibrations, money, lengthens life, promotes fertility, preserves health, and instils courage, physical strength.

**Quartz (Clear):** stone of power, produces naturally balanced energy field, used to amplify psychic energy and thoughts, harmony, activates and clears energy centres. A multi-purpose healing stone, aids in visualization.

**Quartz:** (Blue) peace and tranquility; (Green) prosperity, stimulate creativity; (Herkimer) substitute for diamonds; (Smoky) mood elevator, grounding stone, overcomes depression and negative emotions.

**Quartz (Rose):♥,** emotional harmony, sexuality, fidelity, beauty, kindness, compassion, and loving kindness. Its healing powers works on resolving painful emotions. Promotes self-love, forgiveness, increases fertility, gentle love.

**Ruby:** *P,* symbolizes passion, powerful at magnifying and intensifying emotions both positive and negative, increase courage and overcome difficult situations. Nobility, spiritual wisdom, health and knowledge, bliss, wealth, power, joy, anti-nightmare.

**Sapphire:** *H, ♥,* Creates a crystal clear mental clarity, meditation, peace, defensive magic, power, increased wealth and money.

**Silver:** enhances brain functions, aids circulation, relieves stress, emotional balance, excellent energy conductor.

**Tiger-eyes:** *P, L,* optimism, and creativity. Money, courage and confidence, promotes energy flow, strengthens conviction, beneficial for weak or sick.

**Topaz:** *H, P,* promotes individuality, confidence in trusting one's decisions, promotes expression of ideas, creates changes, wealth and health, weight loss, and relieves depression, anger, fear and disturbing emotions.

**Tourmaline:** *C,♥,* friendship, money, business, health, peace, energy. (Pink) draws love and friendship, promotes sympathy towards others; (Red) protective rituals, promotes courage and strengthens the will; (Green) money and business success, stimulates creativity; (Blue) de-stress, peace and restful sleep; (Black) grounding, earthly energy, protective, absorbs negativity; (Watermelon)♥, balances projective and receptive energies, attraction.

**Turquoise:** *H, L,♥,* protective stone, builds strength, aids communication, peace of mind, emotional balance. Turquoise is the ancient absorber of negativity, and highly guarded by Native Americans. Balancing and healing stone, and brings energy into alignment. Wealth and happiness, friendship, promotes courage, travel protection, increases beauty, and prevents migraines.

**Zircon:** *H, P, ♥,* beauty, peace, sexual energy; (Yellow) increases sexual energy or attracts love, drives away depression, increases alertness, business success; (Orange) increases beauty, stills fears, guards against injury, safeguards against theft; (Red) increases riches, guards against injuries, protective, vitalizes body, heals, draws pain from body; (Brown) grounding, centering, wealth and money spells; (Green) money spells.

# Meditations

# A New Direction

1. Journaling: Journal where you are in your life now and where you would like to be. Date the entry. Elaborate the feelings you want to feel in your new life. Write down all the things you want to release including emotions, feelings or happenings. Write down these feelings on separate small pieces of paper. This is all about endings to begin again.
2. Pray or find sayings or affirmations for new beginnings and for these beginnings to develop easily.
3. New moons, morning (sunrise), first of the month, fall solstice are symbolic for beginnings.
4. Face the west (spiritual renewal) if possible and have something yellow (renewal) which symbolizes newness.
5. Wash your hands or take a shower/bath and wash or cleanse anything else you are using.
6. Light a white candle and/or burn incense to disperse any energies.
7. If using crystals, amber (time, cycles and symbolic of life) is for renewal and endings.

**The Meditation:**

1. Light the white candle and place in a larger vessel which contains a small amount of water; face the west and sit in a circle which contains your crystals and your sayings/affirmations. Sit close to a window so you can observe the moonless sky.
2. Hold all your separate pieces of paper listing what you want to release. Open each one separately and read them. Accept that it is the time of endings now, fold the paper up and then burn them on your candle and let the ashes drop in the vessel below. Continue

until each of the pieces of paper has burned. Sit with the ashes and contemplate what you have released.

3. Take 3 breaths lengthening the exhalation with each repetition. Allow yourself to relax with each breath. Read your sayings or affirmations and repeat several times. Rest with how these sayings make you feel.

4. Read your journal and all the things you want to change in your life and how you want to feel. Imagine them happening and your feelings changing. Rest with these feelings.

5. Open yourself for many new feelings and changes beyond what you have wished for.

6. Take 3 breaths and feel yourself changing with the newness of your feelings. Finish your meditation. Stand in the middle of your circle and say a closing prayer or saying as you complete your meditation. Snub out your candle and return your crystals to their place. Throw out the water and the ashes. Take a final 3 breaths.

7. Repeat as necessary whenever you desire.

# Celebrations – Time

Celebrate the time of day. Meditations don't need to be long and drawn out. When you wake up in the morning, celebrate the fact that a new day has begun.

1. Open your eyes, stretching and yawning. Acknowledge that the day is new and fresh and so is your life.
2. Roll over, sit up and swing your feet to the floor and plant them flat on the floor as if you are planting new shoots ready to carry you forward.
3. Stand up and feel yourself ready to meet the day and everything that the day will bring. Feel excited and happy about your feelings.
4. Open the curtains, blinds or doors and let in the new fresh day/energy. Say good day to your day breathing deeply with it and let it fill your lungs and body.
5. Do your morning preparations, eat breakfast, dress and feel the newness of all of these movements.
6. Go into the day and raise your face to the sun and sky every chance you get. Seek out the sun and where it is in the sky as often as possible to see its journey and yours.
7. Celebrate the middle of the day. Close your eyes; think of the apex of your day; take a complete breath and release it; open your eyes; and celebrate where you are.
8. At the end of the day, acknowledge your day and what has transpired. Eat your meal and appreciate the difference between this meal and your breakfast at the beginning of the day.
9. Unwind yourself and let go. This is the time to relax, stretch and feel the fulfillment of the time you have spent during the day.
10. Celebrate endings. Do your nightly preparations, cleansing the day from you. If you can, look out into the night sky and see if

the stars or moon are visible. Spend a moment with them taking several slow complete breaths.

11. Prepare your bed and realize how comfortable and restful you will be. Pull the covers down, stretch and release, and then sit on the bed. Plant your feet on the ground, release each foot consciously as you roll onto the bed. Pull the covers over and close the lights.

12. Find your comfort on the bed and take several soft breaths opening and closing your eyes slowly. Yawn and sigh releasing your breath with a long expression of letting go. Relax your body completely and let the day go.

# Final Thoughts

In Defining your Space, I talked about using helpers to make your meditations interesting and fresh. Don't be afraid of them. At times you might just want to sit quietly and not accessorize and that is perfectly alright. But other times, you might want to use whatever helpers you're comfortable with and what feels effective. It is about learning and accessorizing what you do. It is the difference between a meal that is take-out or a great home-cooked meal. Make it an event and time and time again, you will find new ways to bring exciting new interests to your practice.

Enjoy what you do and how you make your practice and life interesting. Enjoy them and then eventually let them go because it is all about you.

Enjoy your journey.

# Glossary of Meditations

#1 Physical Body; #2 Awareness; #3 Relaxation; #4 The Hectic Life; #5 The Mental Body
5 Senses #5
Breathing #1
Breathing #2
Breathing #3
Chair Meditation #3
Chair Meditation #4
Knocking/Tapping #4
Laying Pose – Beginning #1
Laying Pose – Beginning #2
Laying Pose – Beginning #3
Laying Pose – Breathing #5
Laying Pose – Right/Left #5
Laying Pose – Stretching #1
Laying Pose – Stretching #2
Laying Pose – Stretching #3
Mental Labyrinth #5
Positive Thoughts #5
Relaxation #5
Relaxation Techniques #5
Sitting and Thinking #5
Sitting Pose – Beginning #1
Sitting Pose – Beginning #2
Sitting Pose – Beginning #3
Sitting Pose – Breathing #4
Sitting Pose – Isolating #4
Sitting Pose – Relaxation #1
Sitting Pose – Relaxation #2

Sitting Pose – Relaxation #3
Sitting Pose – Stretching #1
Sitting Pose – Stretching #2
Sitting Pose – Stretching #3
Sitting Pose #4
Sitting Using Your Chair & Desk #4
Standing Pose – Awareness #4
Standing Pose – Balancing #1
Standing Pose – Balancing #2
Standing Pose – Balancing #3
Standing Pose – Beginning #1
Standing Pose – Beginning #2
Standing Pose – Beginning #3
Standing Pose – Breathing #4
Standing Pose – Isolating #4
Standing Pose – Stretching #1
Standing Pose – Stretching #2
Standing Pose – Stretching #3
Stretching #4
Stroking Off Energy #5
Vision Quest Meditation #5
Walking Meditation #1
Walking Meditation #3
Walking the Labyrinth #2